Dolly Parton

A Journey Through the Life of a Country Legend

Emma Christian

All rights reserved.

No part of this publication may be reproduced, distributed or transmitted in any form or by any means, including photocopying, recording, or other electrical or mechanical methods, without the prior written permission, except in the case of brief quotations, embodied in critical reviews and certain other non-commercial uses permitted by copyright law.

Copyright© Emma Christian 2025

TABLE OF CONTENTS

Chapter 1: Smoky Mountain Roots
Chapter 2: The Girl with the Golden Voice
Chapter 3: Breaking Into Nashville
Chapter 4: "9 to 5"—Dolly's Leap into Hollywood
Chapter 5: Building Dreams—Dolly's Business Empire and Heart for Giving
Chapter 6: Still Shining—Dolly Parton's Recent Projects and Cultural Influence
Chapter 7: A Heart as Big as the World—Dolly Parton's Global Philanthropy
Chapter 8: The Woman Behind the Legend—Dolly Parton's Personal Life and Relationships
Chapter 9: Faith, Family, and Fierce Individuality

Chapter 10: The Legend Lives On

Chapter 1: Smoky Mountain Roots

In the heart of the Great Smoky Mountains, where the mist clings to the trees and the air smells of pine and earth, a little girl named Dolly Rebecca Parton was born on January 19, 1946. Her birthplace was a one-room cabin in Locust Ridge, Tennessee—a place so modest that her father paid the doctor who delivered her with a sack of cornmeal.

Dolly was the fourth of twelve children born to Robert Lee Parton, a hardworking farmer and construction worker, and Avie Lee Parton, a homemaker with a heart full of songs and stories. The Parton family didn't have much in terms of material wealth, but their home was rich with love, faith, and music.

The cabin had no electricity or running water. The children slept three or four to a bed, and meals were simple—often beans, cornbread, and whatever vegetables they could grow. Yet, Dolly remembers her childhood fondly, filled with laughter, storytelling, and singing.

Music was woven into the fabric of daily life. Avie Lee taught her children old Appalachian ballads passed down through generations. Dolly's grandfather, a preacher, introduced her to gospel music at church, where she first performed publicly at the age of six.

By the time she was seven, Dolly had fashioned her first guitar from an old mandolin and fishing line. Recognizing her passion, her uncle bought her a real guitar when she was eight. She began writing songs, pouring her experiences and emotions into lyrics that would later resonate with millions.

At ten, Dolly started performing on local radio and television programs in Knoxville, Tennessee. Her talent was undeniable, and by thirteen, she had recorded her first single, "Puppy Love," and appeared at the Grand Ole Opry, where she met Johnny Cash, who encouraged her to follow her instincts.

Despite the hardships of poverty, Dolly's upbringing in the Smoky Mountains instilled in her a deep appreciation for family, faith, and the power of music. These early experiences shaped the woman she would become—a symbol of resilience, creativity, and generosity.

These humble beginnings laid the foundation for Dolly Parton's extraordinary journey from the hills of Tennessee to the stages of the world.

Chapter 2: The Girl with the Golden Voice

It was 1964. The morning sun hadn't yet warmed the foggy hills when Dolly Parton stood at the tiny bus stop in

Sevierville, Tennessee. She was eighteen years old, clutching a worn suitcase and a dream as wide as the Smoky Mountains behind her. Her family, including her mama and several siblings, had gathered to say goodbye. There were hugs, tears, and soft words of encouragement.

"I'll make you proud," she told her mother, trying to hold back her own tears. Then she climbed onto the Greyhound bus that would take her to Nashville.

That was the day the girl with the golden voice officially left home to chase her dream.

Dolly didn't arrive in Nashville with money, connections, or even a place to stay. But she had what mattered: talent, determination, and a voice that turned heads. Her first stop was her Uncle Bill Owens' house—he was the one who had believed in her from the start. He helped her get small gigs around town and introduced her to people in the music business.

Nashville in the mid-1960s wasn't easy on new artists, especially young women. Many record labels didn't know what to do with a girl who wrote her own songs and had such a strong, unusual voice. At first, they wanted Dolly to sing bubblegum pop music. Monument Records even released a few songs that tried to fit her into that mold.

But the moment Dolly released a song called "Dumb Blonde," everything changed. The lyrics were sharp and cheeky—"Just because I'm blonde, don't think I'm dumb"—and women across America sat up and listened. So did the men.

That song didn't just climb the country charts. It announced that Dolly Parton had arrived.

Her first full album, Hello, I'm Dolly, came out in 1967. It had hits like "Something Fishy" and "The Little Things," and it showed off her songwriting talent. People started to whisper that this young woman wasn't just another pretty face. She was a storyteller with heart.

Not long after the album's release, a big break came that would change Dolly's life forever.

Porter Wagoner was one of the most popular country music stars at the time. He had a syndicated TV show, The Porter Wagoner Show, which aired every weekend in homes across America. He was looking for a new "girl singer," and someone handed him Dolly's record. One listen, and he knew she had something special.

When Dolly stepped onto The Porter Wagoner Show for the first time in 1967, some fans weren't thrilled. They had loved the previous singer, Norma Jean, and didn't think this tiny blonde girl could fill her shoes. But then Dolly opened her mouth and sang.

And people fell in love.

For seven years, Dolly and Porter performed together. They recorded duets like "The Last Thing on My Mind," "Just Someone I Used to Know," and "Daddy Was an Old Time Preacher Man." Their harmonies blended like warm honey and cold sweet tea—different but perfect together.

But behind the scenes, things weren't always smooth. Porter was older, more experienced, and used to being the star. Dolly was rising fast, and that didn't sit well with everyone. She was friendly, charming, and funny on television—but she was also fiercely ambitious.

She didn't just want to be part of someone else's show. She wanted to create her own.

Dolly was writing new songs all the time. Personal songs. Heart songs. Songs that told stories about her childhood, her mama's love, and the struggles of being a woman with dreams in a world that didn't always welcome them. Her song "Coat of Many Colors" told the story of her mama sewing her a patchwork coat out of rags—and how proud she felt wearing it, even when other children teased her.

It wasn't just music. It was memory. And it was powerful.

By 1974, Dolly knew she had to move on. She told Porter she needed to go solo. He didn't take it well.

They fought. He begged her to stay. But Dolly had already made up her mind. And so she did what she does best—she wrote a song.

"I Will Always Love You" was her way of saying goodbye. It wasn't just about business—it was about gratitude, love, and moving on without bitterness.

When she sang it to Porter for the first time, he reportedly had tears in his eyes. He knew it was a perfect song. It went straight to number one and became one of her signature hits.

Years later, Whitney Houston's version of "I Will Always Love You" would become one of the best-selling singles of all time. But it started as a simple, emotional goodbye from a young woman to her mentor.

As Dolly stepped into her solo career, she didn't hesitate. She released hit after hit—"Jolene," "Love Is Like a Butterfly," "The Bargain Store." Her albums were rich with stories, and her voice carried them like wind through the holler.

But it wasn't just her sound that drew people in—it was her spirit. Dolly had a way of being fully herself. She didn't hide her big hair, her makeup, her flashy clothes, or her thick accent. She leaned into it.

"I'm not offended by all the dumb blonde jokes," she once said, laughing. "Because I know I'm not dumb. And I also know that I'm not blonde."

That was the magic. Dolly was funny and wise. She made people laugh, then turned around and broke their hearts with a ballad.

She knew how to connect.

Behind the scenes, Dolly was also smart. Very smart.

She made business deals that gave her ownership of her own songs. She made sure she had control over her image, her publishing rights, and her future. In an industry where artists—especially women—were often treated like disposable products, Dolly made herself the boss.

It wasn't easy. People underestimated her constantly. But she kept smiling, kept singing, and kept climbing.

By the end of the 1970s, Dolly wasn't just a country star. She was a household name.

She still kept her roots close. Every time she went back home to Sevier County, the whole town would light up. She didn't forget where she came from. In fact, she told people about it every chance she got.

She talked about her big family, her tiny cabin, and the love that carried her through. She reminded the world that success wasn't about forgetting your past—it was about honoring it.

Dolly Parton never tried to become someone else. She just became more of herself.

And people loved her for it.

Chapter 3: Breaking Into Nashville

When Dolly stepped off the bus in Nashville, her feet hit the ground like she had stepped into her future. The city was noisy, hot, and full of strangers, but to her, it felt like home. She was just 18, carrying only a guitar, a small suitcase, and dreams bigger than the Smoky Mountains she left behind.

But Nashville wasn't waiting to roll out the red carpet. The music business didn't care where you came from or how sweet your voice was. You had to prove yourself, and Dolly knew it. She didn't waste time. That very first day in the city, she started knocking on doors—music publishers, radio stations, record labels—anyone who would listen.

She didn't have a manager or agent. She had her uncle, Bill Owens, who believed in her more than anyone else. He had driven her to gigs back home and helped her write songs.

Now, he helped her hustle through the streets of Nashville, guitar in hand.

They played anywhere they could—small shows, lounges, and local radio spots. And all the while, Dolly kept writing songs, dozens of them. She poured her heart into every lyric—songs about her childhood, her family, her faith, and her fears. Some were sad, some were funny, and all of them were hers.

Still, most record labels didn't know what to do with her. She was too country for pop, too bold for background singing. One label finally gave her a shot—**Monument Records**—but they didn't understand who she was. They tried to mold her into a pop singer, dressing her up and giving her light, fluffy songs to sing.

But Dolly wasn't light or fluffy. She was full of fire.

Her first few singles didn't do much. She could feel the walls closing in—she'd come all this way, worked so hard, and it wasn't clicking.

Then she recorded **"Dumb Blonde"**—a sassy, sharp, country song that told the world not to judge her by her looks. "Just because I'm blonde," she sang, "don't think I'm dumb, 'cause this dumb blonde ain't nobody's fool."

The song took off. Country radio picked it up, and people started asking: "Who's that little blonde girl with the big voice?" Monument Records finally realized what Dolly had known all along—she wasn't meant to be anyone but herself.

And the world was finally ready for Dolly Parton.

Around the same time, another door opened. A big one.

Porter Wagoner, a country music star with a slick pompadour and rhinestone suits, was looking for a new female singer for his television show. The Porter Wagoner Show was watched by millions of people every weekend. It was a golden opportunity—but it came with a price.

Dolly would have to replace **Norma Jean**, a singer who fans loved deeply. When Porter picked Dolly, she was excited—but also nervous. She knew the audience might not welcome her with open arms.

And they didn't. Not right away.

When Dolly first appeared on the show in 1967, she could feel the cold shoulders from the crowd. People wrote letters begging Porter to bring Norma Jean back. But Dolly smiled through it, stood tall, and sang her heart out every week.

Slowly, things began to change. People couldn't ignore her voice. Or her kindness. Or the way she could tell a story in three verses that made you feel like you lived it yourself.

Within a few months, fans started warming up. Within a year, they loved her.

Dolly and Porter became a hit duo. They released duet after duet—**"The Last Thing on My Mind," "Just Between You and Me," "Daddy Was an Old Time Preacher Man."** Their harmonies were smooth, and their stage banter felt like two old friends trading stories.

But behind the scenes, the story wasn't so smooth.

Porter was older. He was the boss of the show. He saw himself as Dolly's mentor—and he was, at first. But Dolly was growing faster than anyone expected. People weren't just tuning in for Porter anymore. They were tuning in for Dolly.

And that started to cause tension.

Dolly loved Porter, but she didn't want to stay in his shadow forever. She had plans—big ones. She wanted to write, record, tour, and build something of her own. And she knew she'd have to leave the show to do that.

Still, leaving wasn't easy. It wasn't just business. Porter had been like a big brother to her. He'd given her a shot when others wouldn't. So she didn't just walk away. She wrote a song instead.

A goodbye song.

"I Will Always Love You."

She sang it to Porter in his office, just the two of them. As her voice filled the room, soft and sweet and full of feeling, tears rolled down Porter's cheeks. He knew she meant every word.

"You can go," he told her when the song was done. "But you better record that song first."

She did. And it became one of her most famous songs ever.

Leaving The Porter Wagoner Show was the turning point in Dolly's life. It was the moment she took control.

She signed a new record deal. She started making music that was all her own. Songs like:

- **"Jolene"** — A woman begging another not to steal her man.

- **"Love Is Like a Butterfly"** — A gentle tune about love's fragile beauty.

- **"Coat of Many Colors"** — A story from her childhood, about a patchwork coat her mother made and the pride she felt wearing it, even when kids made fun of her.

"Coat of Many Colors" wasn't just a song. It was a message. Dolly was telling people: I've known hard times. I've known love. And I've never been ashamed of where I came from.

The song became one of her most beloved hits.

The 1970s were a rocket ride for Dolly. She was on TV, on the radio, in magazines. Her big hair got higher. Her voice got stronger. And people started calling her something new: a star.

But she never let it get to her head.

She still called home every week. She still sang about her mama, her faith, and her mountain roots. And she still said "thank you" every chance she got.

Breaking into Nashville hadn't been easy. It had taken grit, kindness, and a whole lot of music. But Dolly Parton did it her way—with honesty, humor, and heart.

Chapter 4: "9 to 5"—Dolly's Leap into Hollywood

In the late 1970s, Dolly Parton was already a country music sensation, known for her distinctive voice, heartfelt songwriting, and vibrant personality. However, she was ready to explore new horizons and challenge herself in unfamiliar territories. Hollywood beckoned, and Dolly was eager to answer the call.

Her opportunity came with the 1980 comedy film 9 to 5, a story about three working women who take on their oppressive boss. The film starred Jane Fonda, Lily Tomlin, and marked Dolly's acting debut. Portraying Doralee Rhodes, a secretary often misunderstood because of her looks, Dolly brought authenticity and charm to the role, drawing from her own experiences.

On set, Dolly's natural talent shone through. Despite being new to acting, she impressed her co-stars and the crew with her professionalism and charisma. Her performance was both comedic and heartfelt, resonating with audiences nationwide.

But Dolly didn't stop at acting; she also contributed to the film's music. She wrote and performed the title song, "9 to 5," which became an anthem for working individuals. The song's catchy rhythm and relatable lyrics struck a chord, propelling it to the top of the Billboard Hot 100 chart in 1981 .

The film itself was a massive success, grossing over $103 million and becoming the second highest-grossing film of 1980 . It not only showcased Dolly's versatility but also highlighted issues of workplace inequality, making it a cultural touchstone.

Dolly's venture into Hollywood with 9 to 5 was more than just a career move; it was a statement. She proved that she could transcend genres and mediums, all while staying true to herself. This chapter in her life marked the beginning of a new era, one where Dolly Parton became not just a country music icon, but a beloved figure in American pop culture.

Chapter 5: Building Dreams— Dolly's Business Empire and Heart for Giving

By the 1980s, Dolly Parton had already become a household name in country music. Her songs were topping charts, and her voice was recognized across the nation. But Dolly's ambitions extended beyond the stage and recording studio. She envisioned creating spaces and programs that would bring joy, education, and inspiration to others, especially in her beloved East Tennessee.

Dollywood: A Dream Realized

In 1986, Dolly partnered with Herschend Family Entertainment to transform a small amusement park in Pigeon Forge, Tennessee, into Dollywood. This wasn't just a business venture; it was a heartfelt tribute to her roots. Dollywood combined thrilling rides with Appalachian culture, featuring crafts, music, and storytelling that celebrated the Smoky Mountains' heritage. The park quickly became a major attraction, drawing millions of visitors annually.

Over the years, Dollywood expanded to include a water park, resort hotels, and dinner theaters. Each addition reflected Dolly's commitment to family-friendly entertainment and her desire to create jobs and boost the local economy. In 2025, Dollywood celebrated its 40th anniversary, marking four decades of success and community impact.

Imagination Library: Spreading the Love of Reading

Inspired by her father's inability to read, Dolly launched the Imagination Library in 1995. The program aimed to foster a love of reading among children by mailing them free, age-appropriate books monthly from birth until they started school. What began in Sevier County, Tennessee, grew into a global initiative. By 2025, the Imagination Library had distributed over 270 million books across the United States, Canada, the United Kingdom, Australia, and Ireland.

Dolly often expressed that being called "The Book Lady" by children brought her immense joy, surpassing even her musical accolades. The program's success highlighted her dedication to education and her belief in the transformative power of literacy.

The Dollywood Foundation: Philanthropy in Action

Beyond the Imagination Library, Dolly's philanthropic efforts extended through the Dollywood Foundation, established in 1988. The foundation initially focused on reducing high school dropout rates in Sevier County. One notable initiative was the Buddy Program, where Dolly promised $500 to each student who graduated high school, provided they paired up and supported each other to stay in school. This program significantly decreased dropout rates and demonstrated Dolly's innovative approach to community challenges.

In response to the devastating wildfires in the Smoky Mountains in 2016, Dolly established the My People Fund. The fund provided $1,000 per month for six months to families who lost their homes, totaling over $12 million in aid. This swift action showcased her deep connection to her community and her commitment to helping those in need.

Expanding the Brand: Entertainment Ventures

Dolly's entrepreneurial spirit led her to explore various entertainment avenues. She opened dinner theaters like Dolly Parton's Stampede and Pirates Voyage, offering guests a blend of dining and live performances. These ventures not only entertained but also created jobs and boosted tourism in their respective locations.

In 2025, Dolly announced the opening of a new Pirates Voyage Dinner & Show in Panama City Beach, Florida. The attraction features elaborate performances with aerialists, divers, and singers around a massive indoor water stage, further cementing her status as a visionary in family entertainment.

A Legacy of Giving and Innovation

Dolly's ventures, both philanthropic and business, are rooted in her genuine desire to uplift others. Her initiatives have provided educational resources, economic opportunities, and cultural enrichment to countless individuals. She has received numerous accolades for her efforts, including the 2022 Carnegie Medal of Philanthropy, recognizing her outstanding charitable contributions. Vogue

Through her unwavering commitment to her community and her innovative approach to business and philanthropy, Dolly Parton has built a legacy that transcends music. Her life's work serves as an inspiration, demonstrating how passion, empathy, and determination can create lasting positive change.

Chapter 6: Still Shining—Dolly Parton's Recent Projects and Cultural Influence

Dolly Parton, a name synonymous with country music, has continually reinvented herself, embracing new projects and expanding her influence beyond music. In recent years, she has embarked on ventures that showcase her versatility and commitment to storytelling, education, and entertainment.

Threads: My Songs in Symphony

In 2025, Dolly introduced "Threads: My Songs in Symphony," a multimedia symphonic storytelling experience. This innovative project features orchestral renditions of her iconic songs, accompanied by visual narratives that delve into the stories behind the music. The premiere performance took place with the Nashville Symphony on March 20, 2025, and is set to tour with orchestras worldwide, bringing Dolly's music to new audiences in a unique format.

Pirates Voyage Dinner & Show

Expanding her entertainment empire, Dolly opened the Pirates Voyage Dinner & Show in Panama City Beach, Florida, in May 2025. This immersive attraction features aerialists, divers, and singers performing around a massive indoor water stage, offering guests a blend of dining and live entertainment. The show includes battles between pirate crews, pyrotechnics, and an original song by Dolly herself, highlighting her flair for spectacular productions.

Children's Literature: Billy the Kid Series

Dolly continued her foray into children's literature with the release of "Billy the Kid Dances His Heart Out," the third installment in her Billy the Kid series. The book follows her beloved god-dog, Billy, as he takes up dancing lessons to prepare for Dolly's Doggy Dance Pawty. The story explores themes of self-confidence and perseverance, aiming to make reading enjoyable and meaningful for children and their parents.

Educational Initiatives: Partnership with Belmont University

Dolly expanded her partnership with Belmont University through the Dolly U program, offering students hands-on experience in the music industry. In 2025, four new courses were introduced, providing insights into Dolly's various projects, including the production of a behind-the-scenes documentary related to her autobiographical musical. Nine students received paid fellowships, working directly with the production team as they prepared for the musical's Broadway debut.

Personal Tributes: "If You Hadn't Been There"

In March 2025, Dolly released "If You Hadn't Been There," a heartfelt tribute to her late husband, Carl Dean, who passed away earlier that month. The song reflects on the profound impact Dean had on Dolly's life and career, expressing gratitude for his unwavering support and love throughout their marriage. The single debuted at number 21 on the UK Singles Sales chart, resonating with fans worldwide.

Cultural Influence and Legacy

Dolly Parton's influence extends beyond her musical achievements. She has become a symbol of empowerment, resilience, and kindness, connecting with people from all walks of life. Her ability to blend authenticity with innovation has solidified her status as a unifying figure in popular culture.

Through her recent projects, Dolly continues to inspire and entertain, demonstrating that her creative spirit remains as vibrant as ever. Her endeavors in music, literature, education, and entertainment reflect a commitment to storytelling and a desire to make a positive impact on the world.

Chapter 7: A Heart as Big as the World—Dolly Parton's Global Philanthropy

Dolly Parton is more than a country music legend; she is a beacon of generosity whose philanthropic efforts have touched lives across the globe. From her humble beginnings in the Smoky Mountains to her expansive charitable initiatives, Dolly's commitment to giving back is as profound as her musical legacy.

Seeds of Generosity

Dolly's philanthropic journey was inspired by her father, Robert Lee Parton, who, despite being unable to read or write, possessed immense wisdom and kindness. This personal connection to literacy challenges fueled her passion for education and laid the foundation for her future charitable endeavors.

The Dollywood Foundation

Established in 1988, the Dollywood Foundation began with a focus on reducing high school dropout rates in Sevier County, Tennessee. Through initiatives like the Buddy Program, which offered financial incentives to students who graduated, the foundation achieved remarkable success, significantly lowering dropout rates. Over time, the foundation expanded its reach, supporting various educational and community programs.

Imagination Library: A Global Literacy Movement

In 1995, Dolly launched the Imagination Library, a program that mails free, age-appropriate books to children from birth until they begin school. What started in Sevier County has grown into a global initiative, distributing over 200 million books to children in the United States, Canada, the United Kingdom, Australia, and Ireland. The program's impact is profound, fostering a love for reading and learning in millions of children worldwide.

Disaster Relief and Community Support

Dolly's compassion extends to disaster relief efforts. In response to the devastating wildfires in the Great Smoky Mountains in 2016, she established the My People Fund, providing $1,000 monthly to affected families for six months, totaling over $12 million in aid. Her swift action and substantial support exemplify her deep commitment to her community.Them

Healthcare Contributions

During the COVID-19 pandemic, Dolly donated $1 million to Vanderbilt University Medical Center, contributing to the development of the Moderna vaccine. Her support for healthcare initiatives underscores her dedication to improving lives through science and medicine.

Support for Education and Scholarships

Beyond literacy, Dolly has funded numerous scholarships, providing opportunities for students to pursue higher education. Her secret scholarship fund has supported over 1,000 students, reflecting her belief in the transformative power of education.

Advocacy for Equality and Inclusion

Dolly is a vocal advocate for LGBTQ+ rights, supporting marriage equality and opposing discriminatory legislation. Her inclusive stance promotes acceptance and equality, resonating with diverse communities.

Global Recognition and Awards

Dolly's philanthropic efforts have earned her numerous accolades, including the Carnegie Medal of Philanthropy and the PEACE Through Music Award. These honors recognize her unwavering commitment to making the world a better place through her charitable work.

A Legacy of Love and Giving

Dolly Parton's philanthropic journey is a testament to the impact one individual can have on the world. Her initiatives have provided education, relief, and hope to countless individuals, embodying a legacy of love and generosity that transcends borders.

Chapter 8: The Woman Behind the Legend—Dolly Parton's Personal Life and Relationships

Dolly Parton, the iconic country music star, is celebrated not only for her musical talents but also for her deep personal relationships and unwavering values. Beyond the glitz and glamour, Dolly's life is a tapestry woven with love, faith, and resilience.

A Humble Beginning

Born on January 19, 1946, in Locust Ridge, Tennessee, Dolly Rebecca Parton was the fourth of twelve children in a modest family. Her father, Robert Lee Parton, was a sharecropper and construction worker, while her mother, Avie Lee Owens, managed the household and nurtured their children's musical inclinations. Growing up in a one-room cabin, the Parton family's life was filled with love, music, and faith, despite financial hardships.

A Lifelong Love: Carl Dean

At 18, Dolly met Carl Thomas Dean outside a Nashville laundromat. Their connection was immediate, leading to a private wedding ceremony in Ringgold, Georgia, on May 30, 1966. Carl, a businessman who owned an asphalt-laying company, preferred a life away from the spotlight, rarely accompanying Dolly to public events. Despite his reclusive nature, their bond remained strong, characterized by mutual respect and deep affection.

Their nearly 60-year marriage was a testament to enduring love. Dolly often spoke of Carl's unwavering support, describing him as her anchor amidst the whirlwind of fame. In March 2025, Carl passed away at the age of 82, leaving Dolly to navigate life without her beloved partner. She candidly shared her grief, referring to the transition as a "big adjustment," and released a heartfelt tribute song titled "If You Hadn't Been There" to honor his memory.

Family Ties

Dolly's family has always been central to her life. Her siblings—Willadeene, David Wilburn, Coy Denver, Robert Lee (Bobby), Stella Mae, Cassie Nan, Randle Huston (Randy), Larry Gerald, twins Floyd Estel and Frieda Estelle, and Rachel Ann—each hold a special place in her heart. Several of them pursued musical careers, with Stella and Randy achieving notable success. Dolly's close-knit family provided a foundation of support and inspiration throughout her journey.

Aunt Granny and Godmother

Though Dolly and Carl never had children of their own, they played significant roles in the lives of their nieces and nephews, earning Dolly the affectionate nickname "Aunt Granny."

Additionally, Dolly is the godmother of pop star Miley Cyrus, the daughter of Billy Ray Cyrus. Their relationship is marked by mutual admiration and support, with Dolly often offering guidance and encouragement to Miley as she navigates her own career in the spotlight.

Faith and Resilience

Dolly's Christian faith has been a cornerstone of her life, providing strength during challenging times. In the 1980s, she faced a personal crisis following a partial hysterectomy, leading to a period of depression. Dolly credits her faith and the companionship of her dog, Popeye, for helping her overcome these dark moments. She and Carl even built a chapel on their property in Brentwood, Tennessee, where they would pray together, reinforcing their spiritual bond.

A Private Sanctuary

Despite her public persona, Dolly cherishes her privacy. Her home in Brentwood serves as a sanctuary, a place where she can relax, reflect, and find solace. She enjoys simple pleasures like cooking, reading, and spending time with loved ones. This balance between her public and private life has been crucial in maintaining her well-being and authenticity.

Conclusion

Dolly Parton's personal life is a rich tapestry of enduring love, strong family bonds, and unwavering faith. Her relationships, particularly with her late husband Carl Dean, exemplify a deep commitment to love and mutual respect. Through life's triumphs and trials, Dolly remains grounded, drawing strength from her roots and the people who have shaped her journey.

Chapter 9: Faith, Family, and Fierce Individuality

Dolly Parton's life is a harmonious blend of deep-rooted faith, unwavering family bonds, and an unapologetic embrace of individuality. These core values have not only shaped her personal journey but have also resonated with fans worldwide, making her an enduring icon.

Faith: The Guiding Light

From her earliest days in the Smoky Mountains, Dolly's life was steeped in faith. Raised in a Pentecostal household, her grandfather, Jake Owens, was a preacher, and church was a central part of family life. This spiritual foundation instilled in her a profound belief in God's presence and guidance.

Dolly often refers to her faith as a "guiding light," influencing every aspect of her life and career. She has stated, "My faith impacts everything I do because I do believe that, through God, all things are possible." This belief has been a source of strength during life's challenges, including health issues and personal losses.

While she identifies as spiritual rather than strictly religious, Dolly's faith remains central to her identity. She emphasizes love, compassion, and forgiveness, often expressing that if God can forgive, so should we. Her music, philanthropy, and personal interactions reflect these values, offering hope and inspiration to many.

Family: The Heartbeat of Her Life

Family has always been at the heart of Dolly's world. As the fourth of twelve children, she grew up in a close-knit household where love and music were abundant, even if material possessions were scarce. Her parents, Avie Lee and Robert Lee Parton, instilled in their children the importance of hard work, faith, and supporting one another.

Dolly's siblings have played significant roles in her life and career. Her sister Stella pursued her own music career, while others have collaborated with Dolly on various projects. Despite her fame, Dolly remains deeply connected to her family, often referring to them in interviews and songs.

Though she and her late husband, Carl Dean, did not have children, Dolly embraced the role of "Aunt Granny" to her nieces and nephews, and she is the godmother to singer Miley Cyrus. Her nurturing spirit extends beyond her immediate family, evident in her philanthropic efforts focused on children's literacy and well-being.

Fierce Individuality: Embracing Her True Self

Dolly Parton's individuality is as iconic as her music. From her distinctive fashion choices to her candid personality, she has always embraced her uniqueness with confidence. She once remarked, "It takes a lot of money to look this cheap," highlighting her self-deprecating humor and awareness of her image.

Her style, characterized by flamboyant outfits and big hair, challenges conventional norms and celebrates self-expression. Dolly's authenticity resonates with fans across generations, encouraging them to embrace their true selves without fear of judgment.

Beyond aesthetics, Dolly's individuality shines through her career choices and philanthropic endeavors. She has navigated the entertainment industry on her terms, maintaining creative control over her work and using her platform to advocate for causes close to her heart.

Interweaving Faith, Family, and Individuality

Dolly Parton's life is a testament to the harmonious coexistence of faith, family, and individuality. Her deep spirituality provides a moral compass, guiding her actions and decisions. Her family roots keep her grounded, reminding her of where she came from and the values that shaped her. Her fierce individuality empowers her to break barriers and inspire others to do the same.

In a world that often demands conformity, Dolly stands as a beacon of authenticity. Her journey illustrates that staying true to oneself, while honoring one's faith and family, can lead to a fulfilling and impactful life.

As we reflect on Dolly Parton's remarkable story, we are reminded of the power of embracing our beliefs, cherishing our loved ones, and confidently expressing our individuality. Her legacy continues to inspire, encouraging us all to live with purpose, passion, and authenticity.

Chapter 10: The Legend Lives On

Dolly Parton's legacy is a rich tapestry woven from her contributions to music, culture, feminism, and Southern identity. Her influence spans generations, offering lessons in authenticity, resilience, and compassion.

Musical Innovation and Influence

Dolly's songwriting prowess is evident in classics like "Jolene," "9 to 5," and "I Will Always Love You." Her ability to convey deep emotions through simple lyrics has inspired countless artists across genres. Dolly's music often addresses social issues, with songs like "Just Because I'm a Woman" challenging gender norms in country music.

Cultural Icon and Feminist Symbol

While Dolly has often shied away from labeling herself a feminist, her actions speak volumes. She has consistently advocated for women's rights and empowerment through her music and philanthropy. Her portrayal of strong, independent women in songs and films has challenged traditional gender roles and inspired many.

Embracing Southern Identity

Dolly's Southern roots are integral to her identity. She embraces her Appalachian heritage, often incorporating elements of Southern culture into her work. Her authenticity resonates with audiences, challenging stereotypes and highlighting the richness of Southern traditions.

Philanthropy and Generosity

Beyond her artistic contributions, Dolly's philanthropic efforts have left an indelible mark. Her Imagination Library, which provides free books to children, has distributed over 200 million books worldwide. She has also donated millions to disaster relief and healthcare initiatives, including funding research for the COVID-19 vaccine .

Enduring Influence

Dolly's impact extends beyond her lifetime. Her music continues to inspire new generations, and her values of kindness, authenticity, and resilience serve as guiding principles. As a unifying figure, she bridges cultural and political divides, embodying the power of staying true to oneself.

In reflecting on Dolly Parton's life and legacy, we find a blueprint for living with purpose and compassion. Her story teaches us that embracing our roots, standing up for what we believe in, and giving back to our communities can create a lasting, positive impact.

Made in the USA
Monee, IL
13 May 2025